growing

katie cecilia

Published in 2024 in the UK by
Katie Cecilia.

Kindle Direct Publishing.

Copyright © 2024 Katie Cecilia. All rights reserved.

No part of this publication may be reproduced, stored, or transmitted in any form by any means, electronic, mechanical, photocopying, or otherwise, without the prior written permission of the publisher.

The right of Katie Cecilia to be identified as the author of this work has been asserted by her accordance with the Copyright, Designs, and Patents Act, 1988.

ISBN: 9781805179054

to my inner child who didn't use her voice,
to the woman i will become.

to anyone who is still finding their voice,
to anyone growing too.

to you reading this book,

this one's for *you*.

chapters

daisies (*innocence*) 1

dahlia (*warnings and change*) 14

lily of the valley (*return of happiness*) 42

forget-me-not (*purity and love*) 72

daffodils (*new beginnings*) 96

Daisies
(*innocence*)

growing

i like my writing messy;
the lines are always missing each other.
i like my bedroom tidy,
hiding unfolded clothes in every corner.
i have always been indecisive,
a confident, insecure people-pleaser.
my thoughts are always scattered
from past to future;
i always give too much of myself
and then withdraw, scared that i'll lose her.
agreeing with opinions
that could not be farther from my truth,
thinking overtime
comparing and contrasting
how i am spending my youth.
i am an understood misconception
if you look close enough;
i am a positive-speaking
mental health advocate
trying to convince myself

i am enough.

growing

i owe it to myself to experience this life
as softly as possible.

growing

when we are young, we are taught to align our routines and desires with people our own age. we take classes together. we work together. we eat lunch together. we laugh together. we grow together. until you blink and you're in your twenties, and for the first time in your life, every single person in your age bracket is headed for a sunset that is a different shade of orange to yours. some decide to pack a bag and travel the world. some decide to settle down in their hometown. some decide to find themselves in multiple jobs in multiple cities. some pursue creative passions. some decided at age eleven and stuck to it. some changed their minds ten times over. for the first time, nobody your age is balancing on the same rope as you are. it is scary to worry about not having anything or anyone to hold on to. it can be daunting to be unsure of the road ahead when the lines seem so blurred, but the beauty of being on your own path is that you can never fall off it; you can only be redirected.

growing

i want something different for myself.
slow mornings,
books overflowing my shelves,
working a simple job
that puts my degree to waste,
spending so much time in softness
that i wonder why
i ever idolised burnout in the first place.

growing

i forgive easily
because i don't like making people stay out
in the rain for too long;
they'll catch a chill.
a chill like that stays with you,
so i let them back in
and let them borrow a blanket.
saying i won't be as kind this time,
but i find myself making their bed,
kissing them on the forehead
with a cup of coffee just the way they like.
i spoonfeed my kindness
to the same people
who caused my starvation.
i let them stay warm and safe
in the walls of my heart;
if i didn't, they would catch a chill
the kind that stays with you.

growing

i know there are parts of me that exist
in places that i haven't explored yet.
i can feel it in my bones.
there is an urge i cannot explain
to get on the next flight and just
go
because i know when i get there
she will be waiting for me,
and it will make sense
why i always felt so out of place.

growing

once again, i am a child
sitting by the door
looking out of the window.
waiting
for a gust of wind,
for an apology,
for a look,
for anything, really.
i'm all out of chances,
but i refuse to look away.

what if i miss you?

what if i miss you finally coming home?

growing

from the sweetness of my inner child
and the dirt they threw at me,
i will plant a tree with a view for miles.
i will climb higher
and breathe cleaner air.
i will stay soft.
i will be a safe place for the birds to rest
and the bugs to live in.
i will feed the rabbits,
be shelter for the bears.
i will withstand the weather
because seasons change
and i can bloom again.
my rotted roots will not determine
how far i go.

growing

just because it is all you knew
does not mean it is all you will ever know.

growing

the ceilings that kept you stuck
are not serving you anymore;
they never did.
there is a whole new view out there
waiting for you.
i know how scary the unknown can be,
but facing those fears
will always be worth the liberation
of having the freedom
to be the person you hoped to be
from the very start.

growing

i get excited to tell you things
like a child proudly showing their tenth drawing of the day.
life is more exciting when you have someone
to tell all of the mundane and crazy stories to.

growing

sometimes you meet people in the summer. it is so warm and vibrant it has to be august. sometimes they arrive so fast it causes whiplash and startles your heart to beat faster. sometimes they have rehearsed the comedians and late-night talk shows so they are witty and match your banter. sometimes when it rains, they happen to have an umbrella. sometimes the right words fall from their mouth, and you wonder if they have cherry-picked thoughts from your brain. sometimes there is a rollercoaster of highs and lows, but you stay because of how warm you felt that one august, even though it has been winter for months ever since. sometimes their colours are warning signs. sometimes you can't see who they are because when you put on the rose glasses, everything shows as pink.

Dahlia
(warnings and change)

growing

i want to build a life that
i don't want to run away from.

growing

i thought i knew what i wanted. i thought i knew how. i thought, through some wild transformation, i would have it "together by now". there is so much pressure to have it figured out, but i still struggle with knowing what '*it*' is. there are gaps in my mind that persist, no matter how many friends or places i visit. i'm doing everything i can to make the pieces fit, but is my future self shaking her head and saying, "you'll regret it"? i get ready every morning, put on a t-shirt and jeans i like, and no matter how much work i burn through, i am just 'getting by'. is that all there is? is there something missing? is there even an answer? the dreams i had at 17 are no longer the imagery that my soul calls after. i'm scared to rock the boat. i keep telling myself i should. i don't want to waste my youth on memories of running as fast as i could. they call it growing pains, something none of us can avoid. no matter where i seem to turn, even in the quiet, the twenties are filled with so much noise.

growing

i get silent in big crowds;
my mind does all of the talking for me.
i watch people seamlessly laugh and dance,
unapologetically being themselves.
under my layers, i am just like that;
whispers and giggling hold me back;
"what if" scenarios worry me back into a corner
i am far too comfortable in.
i wonder what it would be like to try
to light up a room,
making my presence known to every face.

i wonder what it would be like to not be afraid to *try*.

growing

it's finally happening—
the beginning of dreading my birthday.
i remember every countdown,
every planning session,
and the beaming smile on my face.
i used to beg my mother for clues,
plan my outfit months in advance,
stargazed about what my new age would lead me to.

somewhere after twenty-one,
those energetic feelings seemed to change;
birthdays now are blowing out the candles
and always feeling the same age.
is it normal to celebrate turning a new leaf
while simultaneously feeling this stuck?
is it just all bad timing, or am i already out of luck?

with the increase of the next number,
i want to claw the clock hands back.
why does it have to be so scary?
why can't i keep feeling excitement like that?

i fixate on every pattern on the cake
with both wonder and fear,
if i will reignite the desire to age again
or if i will feel this way
every year.

growing

i am mad at the world. my alarm didn't sound until way past eight; i burned my breakfast, and now my bus is late. i am mad at the world. the weather sucks, there's nothing good on tv, and all my paychecks do is make ends meet. i am mad at the world. my family dynamics are a mess; my social battery is depleted, but i have plans because extroverted me said "yes." i am mad at the world. my bills are increasing, every situationship is misleading, and so far, my degree has been a waste of tears and reading. i am mad at the world. strangers on the internet are being mean; they say bad things come in threes, but the unlucky raincloud seems to keep pouring down on me. i am mad at the world. i probably will be again. but i will still get out of bed and be hopeful for the next, even on days when everything gets in the way—because as long as i am still here breathing, there is always room for better days.

growing

you're a tornado when you're angry,
tearing up everything in sight.
you texted me to tell me you broke the bathroom sink;
you wouldn't hurt me like that,
but you might.
you have a sweetness
that leaves a bitter aftertaste.
i know you would never hurt me,
but i shared my location in case.
if only my trust in you
didn't make you baby pink,
if only my adoration for you
didn't make me ignore what they think.
it is clear as day
that i am just a toy to you,
but you came all this way to see me,
so i might as well wear the dress you bought;
it would be rude not to.

growing

no matter how the fire looks,
a burn is a burn.
just because you are used to
the way it hurts
does not mean
it is what you deserve.

growing

i tell you it is over
with a quivering lip
and slightly dilated eyes.
you know i'm lying;
the tears only shed to reflect
the open door.
all it would take
is one look and an empty apology
for me to let you back in.
no matter how tall i stand,
you know a breeze is all it takes
to knock me back.
you know me;
you know you are my weakness;
i hate you for that.

growing

i am still waiting for that *click*, for the pieces to fall into place. to have wisdom in hindsight for all the mess i have made. surely there's a shift, something to move so it all makes sense. a chance to collect my traumas and wrongdoings and finally know what to do with all of it. because this can't be all there is—growing old and never growing up. to wrinkle with responsibilities when underneath, i am still that same child searching for safety and love. the adults always seemed to know, and they always made it known that they did. i never realised growing old wasn't growing up, cosplaying in an adult body but still dreaming and feeling, never really leaving who i was as a kid.

growing

fyi, can i just ask
when did everyone start knowing
how to pick a path?
since when did people figure out
who they wanted to be?
out of all the people i've met,
i know myself the least.
stuck in a spiral of panic;
am i lost in translation?
how have they all arrived
when i'm still searching for my destination?
it looks so easy for them.
this confusion is rotting my mind;
surely there are easier routes.
the directions are impossible to find.
my eyes are stinging
as i stare at this blank canvas.
what do i have to do
to be given a map
and innately know
how to understand it?

growing

if you do not know
what you want to do
or where you want to be,
you are one of the lucky ones
because you can travel the world
or have both feet in your hometown.
you can go solo
or rediscover yourself in the crowd.
your path is not predetermined or decided.
you get to choose and change your mind
without breaking a promise or wasting time.
immerse yourself in the unknown.
it is the only way you will grow.

growing

what if the version of myself that i grow into
isn't your type?
and i become
someone you still love
but not someone you like?

growing

judgement always blocks the door when i go to meet myself. she twists and turns stories while comparing me to everybody else. i try to tempt her with the possibility that things can go differently, but she shakes her head, turns me around, and calls me "silly." judgement is in the way of all the things i want to do or say; she makes me think that if i did, they would see me the same way. judgement has me paranoid to never be myself. judgement has me bottling my feelings, reluctant to ask for help. judgement knows that anything i say is glass they will see right through. judgement calls me undeserving of every room i walk into. judgement likes to follow me home; she pokes and prods at every thought so i'm never alone. judgement always blocks the door when i go to meet myself. she twists and turns stories whilst comparing me to everybody else.

growing

i did not mean to leave.
if i am honest, i thought you would
come chasing after me,
banging down every door
with a flower or two.
i just thought that if i took
a few steps back,
the space would suffocate you,
and you would feel the lack
of our late-night calls,
the mundane coffee afternoons,
the way our walls came down,
and i knew everything about you.
i just thought that if i was in the
background
behind the trees,
slightly out of sight,
you would realise, but instead
you found solace in my disappearance
and you left me

behind.

growing

she's out there somewhere, climbing ladders, building different towers, and investing in her creative flair. she is somewhere in the parallel, exploring different patterns and pursuing passions that could've been mine if i had taken another stairwell. she is who i would've been if i had decided on another route, taken the time to review, and changed what talent i could use. when i think of her, i feel greedy for longing for her life and disregarding the blessings that only belong to me. i can't help but be jealous of all the views she gets; all i can do is reminisce about a daydream, staring into the distance. i wonder what could exist if i got to explore all the lives i could have lived.

growing

nobody has ever been more unkind to me
than i have been
to myself.

growing

i am a giver;
pieces of my heart are scattered
across the hands of every person i have ever loved,
even with an empty cup i pour.
when their lights go out,
i give all of my candles and matches away,
even when every time i do,
they set fire to my favourite things.
i am a giver,
especially to those i shouldn't be.

growing

i feel like i'm mourning my twenties whilst i'm experiencing them, as if an older version is fondly remembering and vicariously living through my present moments. it has been drilled into my subconscious that i only get to be in my twenties once, and i unwillingly remind myself of that every single day. i have never been this aware of how slow the days can be and how instant the years go by. i see the smile lines and wrinkles on the adults who raised me; i get teary-eyed when i think about it. every time i heal from something, somewhere else is left cracked, as if i am trying to collect water with my bare hands. i can hold some, but the rest will always run between my fingers. i am not sure what switch has been pressed or who sits in the hidden parts of my mind, but something somewhere can't help but shake me, letting me know how wonderfully fleeting it all is.

growing

i stare out of the window of my nine to five; the blue sky never ceases to remind me of all the life i am missing. all of the dreams that i could be living but are dismissed and suppressed by corporate greed. i want to be out there, anywhere. the clouds glide between the blinds, almost to mock me. just like my youth and the days, they pass me by.

growing

i read all the self-help books
and stopped telling lies,
so why is it still raining?
no matter how hard i try.
my bedroom is still a wreck;
i have cleaned it three times.
today feels exhausting,
and it's only 10:05am.
there is still washing to do
currently on day four.
the air is getting colder.
i don't know what i want anymore.
my heart is pounding
as i sit in the corner of this room.
you used to help me pick the pieces up.
how do i go on without you?

growing

when i miss you, i listen to the playlist we made. i listen to every lyric of every single song like they are your words. i have had it on repeat for the past three days. you only exist when those songs come on. it is the closest i'll ever be to you again.

growing

opinions are not facts.
just because someone thinks
you will never get anywhere
does not mean they are right
because they are usually wrong—
so wrong.
i know with you
they were terribly wrong
because you are going to do fantastically,
aren't you?

growing

sometimes people that we really want don't want us as badly. they realise they can drift, climb, and disappear happily. if they want to go, they will, regardless of the season, and they'll go whether or not you accept their reasons. even when the gate is on its hinges, even when they promised it would be different, they will let you slip through their fingers if they are convinced your memory won't linger. when this happens, it is important that you let them go, not because it's easy and not because they weren't the human embodiment of home. you let them go because you deserve more; you deserve someone to stay without claw marks on the door. you deserve to be chosen, you deserve to be seen, and you deserve someone who wants to be consistent and meet your needs. so when the time comes that their minds desire something else, the only person who you should be concerned about losing is yourself.

growing

just because things aren't turning out how you thought they would doesn't mean that it is bad.
nature has a season of wilting so that it can blossom.
you will blossom too.

growing

i've never met a bigger person, so small.
you should be full of wonder.
baby, you're still growing;
why are you carrying it all?
adult sighs reenacted,
red marks on your shoulders.
who told you that having your needs ignored
was inevitable for getting older?
place them on the ground;
you're missing out on a new view.
all the weight of the world
was never meant to belong to you.

growing

i

am

going

to

make

myself

proud

no

matter

how

much

it

takes

growing

i will create a beautiful life for myself
and you will hear nothing about it.

Lily of the valley

(*return of happiness*)

growing

i keep abandoning myself
for a concept of who i could be.
hours fall away most evenings
at the thought of being anywhere else
or being anyone else.
this body feels like a vessel
merely serving a purpose to carry me
from one place to another,
as if i could discard her
the second i reached somewhere new,

but without her,
i would never reach somewhere new at all.
i should give her more credit
and make a home out of her
instead of a means of transportation.
after all,
she is who i longed to be
before i knew other places existed.

growing

you were never mine to keep—
just some loose change,
a dress i should have returned,
but life got in the way,
so you were thrown in the back of my closet
with the shoes that are slightly too small
and the jacket i promised my mother i would wear.
you were added to the list of things
that should be long gone,
but i held on to the sentimental value
of a moment in time
where picking you made sense.
so maybe i should hand you away
for someone else to wear
to see things in you that i never did.
but you are still there
in the darkness of my closet
for my own selfish reasons,
just in case
you fit perfectly someday.

growing

it hits you
in the middle of doing your grocery shopping,
when you're chatting to an old friend,
doing the laundry,
laughing at a funny video,
and singing along in the car.
as you're trying to get an early night,
when you think you've healed,
when you aren't thinking about it.
life moves on,
the clock ticks,
and it hits you all over again.
acknowledge it,
feel it,
then *let it pass*
because *it will*
and *it does.*

growing

it is 6:56 p.m.
i am rereading our texts.
your hundredth apology,
relieved that i no longer live there,
missing how we would laugh.
it has been far too long for me
to be this emotional.
missing someone feels lonely
as i stare at the cursor,
doubting,
hoping
that you're doing this too.

growing

even when my organs and my bones
have been screaming to leave,
i still feel my heart sinking.
you can know you're on the wrong boat,
but know that you'll miss
the way it glides along the waves
or the views of sunrises it gives you.
you can be sad about a decision
about leaving,
about staying,
or about anything.
even if you know
it is exactly the right decision for you.

growing

it is always better
to walk a path with shaking legs
and an unsure heart
that will lead you to new sunrises
than to stay where you are,
where the wind leaves burns
in the house that never felt like *home*.

growing

i talk to my ceiling about you a lot. i guess that's because it is the only way you are still around. my brain doesn't know how to function without you inhabiting it. if i don't remind myself, i fear i might forget, like you're just another thing that happened. i can't discard something so sacred like that.

growing

i have had unwavering trust
in crooked floorboards before;
forgive me if i am cautious now;
i still have bruised knees.

growing

you are more than what you can offer people. giving is not currency for acceptance of your existence. you are worth it regardless of the fruit you bear. you are worth it because you are here.

growing

i do not regret everything i have worked for—
the blood, sweat, and tears it took to get me here.
but i suppose
i wish someone would have sat me down
in my teen years,
put a curl or two behind my ear,
and told me that the weight i carry
the amount i juggle,
and the titles of my jobs
do not align with my worthiness.
i wish i had been told that
i was worth it anyway.
i wish i was told that i did not need
to overburden or burn myself out

to be worth something.

growing

i have stopped painting you in gold and bright colours
and sweeping your behaviour under the rug
just because of the history we have together.
i no longer make excuses for the way you behave
or fall for your empty promises
just because you look at me that way.
i no longer exist in the delusion where i am convinced
i can love the change out of you.
you used to be covered with hope and forgiveness,
and now i just see right through you
i deserve peace of mind,
communication, and space when i need it.
i deserve soft and welcoming love.
i should not have to break my bones
and disrespect the body that keeps me alive
to deserve it.

growing

i suppose if i had listened to myself,
i would've been painting,
i would've kept learning guitar,
i would've started writing earlier.
i would have been *her*,
not just wished i was.

growing

feelings are multi-facetted;
i can miss you with all i have
while being grateful for the damage you did.
i met a new version of myself;
i healed in ways i never thought i could.
you still live in my heart,
but if i was asked to do it all again,
if i was asked to get my heart broken by you again

i would.

growing

i am sitting on the edge of a mountain
that i fought for decades to be able to be on,
to sit here and embrace the view.
i should feel weightless;
i should feel accomplished,
and i do, in a way.
i guess i am realising
that the motivation to climb
was to prove certain people wrong
who weren't even watching.
is it wrong to want to climb back down?
there is temptation in the jump,
but what if i never land?
i now know the high skylines and stars
are so pretty all the way up here,
but the shades of blue mean nothing to me
if i got here by following the call
of a voice that was never mine to listen to.

growing

deep down,
i am still hopeful that
we find our way back to each other,
waving white flags and smiling.
we will sit in the sun somewhere,
i will tell you about my life.
you'll apologise for the lack of you in it.
we will cry,
and we will heal.
i still hold on to the hope
that time will be on our side.
i still hope
i always have.

growing

i left the door open for people
who will never walk through them again;
i am reminded of this
every time there is a breeze.

growing

rest in peace
to the dreams i never caught
when the opportunity was standing right in front of me.
to the friendships i wish
i would have fought for more.
to the times where my voice was needed
but nobody heard a sound.
to the breathtaking views,
to the people that i have to live without.
to the version of me who gave her heart away
and aligned her thoughts with others
in hopes they would like me,
and it would lead me somewhere someday.
to the life that i could have had
if i didn't stand in my own way.
rest in peace for the time i will never get back
and for everything that was never mine
but i could have had.

growing

i am not a reward for you finally growing into the person you promised me you were. chances have an expiration date. i got on the train. i stopped waiting. your flowers are beautiful, and i am happy for you, but you watched my garden die with a full watering can in your hand. the lack of sun did not make me nocturnal. i found the light again. i bloomed without you, and i will continue to do so.

growing

i won't sugarcoat it; *healing is hard.*

it is days, months, and years of trying and rewiring. it is ten steps forward and seven steps back, and you are questioning your progress, if you can even call it that. it is letting your guard down and risking being hurt. it is learning not to internalise and communicating your feelings with words. it is unlearning behaviours so you don't become a repeat offender; it is accepting your mistakes as you constantly try to do better. it is crying when you need to and letting yourself feel. it is seeing every day as a chance to start again and an opportunity to heal. it is doing what you can to do better where you can; it is trusting that despite countless failed attempts, there will be a time when you won't fall—you'll peacefully land.

growing

the house will stay burning until someone puts out the fire. often times, it takes putting the fire out just so you don't light up the next house you walk into. it can take months and years to fizzle a flame that wasn't started by you. eventually, as you learn how the fires behave, the climate that they are in, and the tricks to manage their temperament, the flame will start to fizzle out. that is not to say that there will never be a house fire again or that you will never see a fire in your life. but once you start knowing how to handle it, it will have less of an effect on you. so eventually, when you find a house with your favourite flowers by the window and a garden for your dog, the wooden panel floors and matches in the kitchen drawer will only remind you of safety.

growing

i avoided pink for years, like a child rejecting their vegetables. i would block out every sight of it, stay inside when the sun would cascade shades across my bedroom, and close the blinds when they would peek through. i masked my natural aura with darker colours and sound-tracked with even darker music because it would have been exhausting to try to be so dainty when i felt so heavy. pink reminded me of the girlhood that i never got to immerse myself in because i was always fighting battles i was born into. it reminded me of softness, a characteristic that was met with judgement and wine stains on the stairs. i wouldn't be able to pinpoint exactly when my perspective shifted; fight or flight is a whirlwind, and memory loss is hereditary. however, i bought a pink flask last week, and recently i started tying pretty bows on my cowboy boots. i am not sure how being healed feels, but this is as close as i have ever gotten.

growing

i need you to let me go; your grip is only leaving bruises. i know you're scared of what will come as a result of the love you'll be losing, but my life should cascade with colour, and for months we have been so dismal. no matter how many times i re-tie our broken strings, we still remain abysmal. this is not an act of spite, revenge, or hate; letting go was inevitable, and unlike last time, my heart isn't able to wait. the act of leaving is rooted in deep care. i still want the world and stars for you; *i just can't be the one to watch you get there.*

growing

i am so tired of gripping onto ancient grudges and traumas, letting them dictate and direct my life. it is exhausting to be continuously paralysed by the anxiety of opinions, outgrowing versions of myself, and regretting in hindsight. i might never forgive, and i might never forget, but i don't want to carry this weight anymore or make decisions that replay old habits. if i do not do the work, i will deny myself entry to rooms and all of the endless possibilities that are waiting and designed for me. the more my eyes peer behind me at closed doors and abandoned paths, the more i'm missing scenery curated for my perception. i don't want to run in circles around pre-existing storytelling and fear. i don't want to blind myself to all of the blessings i could have. i don't want to never meet the best version of myself that i could be because i was so fixated on who i was. those who stole my nights back then should not be entitled to my days years later. it is overwhelming to carry those burdens for such a long time. weight feels heavier the longer that you hold onto it. i have callouses and bruises from mine. deep wounds leave scars, so even at my healthiest, i'll have marks, but going forward, they will not be a reminder of the hurt *but of the beauty and reward of how far i have come.*

growing

i hope i never meet her again—
the version of me that acted out of survival.
i hope i find so much peace
that your number
is not the only one i want to dial.
i hope i travel the world someday,
discovering new places,
seeing things from a different perspective,
and recognising new faces.
i hope i am far away from my hometown
and those people who are stuck in their ways.
the years have thrown me past the sun
while they have stayed the same.
i hope to heal from what has hurt me,
so i am not passing the hurt around.
i hope i continue to breathe
and trust in this new life
i have found.

growing

a soft heart
is the scariest place i could land.
somewhere warm and sweet
with a delicate tone and dry land,
he will think i'm funny,
maybe even pretty.
i'll ask him what he'd like to do,
and he will use those hours getting to know me.
it feels reckless
to place my heart in gentle hands.
it feels risky to tell it all
to someone who'll never understand.
how silly it must sound
to not trust someone honest,
and how stupid it must be
to lock eyes with a blue sky
but have the urge to gravitate
towards storm clouds for safety.

growing

hey,
just so you know,
we are going to get there.
i'm sorry it has taken me so long
to realise that what i was doing
wasn't really what we wanted,
but i heard you
loud and clear.
from here on out
it is you and me
figuring out life
together.

- to my inner child

growing

every time i worry,
it knocks me off my feet.
expecting the worst
and questioning where i am meant to be.
analysing in advance
never seems to help me prepare.
the only way i can know
what will happen
is by walking forward
to get there.

growing

as the days get darker
and the air gets colder,
i hope you are kind to yourself.
some days you will carry the world,
some days you will carry nothing at all,
and you are worth it
on both days
and every day in between.

growing

i will not wish away the person i am now
when it took years of begging and healing
to become her.

growing

Forget me not

(*purity and love*)

growing

who i was
is still not ready
for who i am going to be.
she rattles my bones,
concerned about the fog i am headed towards.
she tells me she cannot prepare me
for a life we have never lived;
she does not know what the rooms contain,
and she is scared of being stung again.
i tell her that the map we once had
does not lead to the destination
that we need to go to now.
i tell her to put her faith in me.
i tell her that i may not know what lies ahead
or have an answer to every question,
but we have always overcome change,
and i trust that as i go,

i will figure it out.

growing

the universe holds both hands out for me with
treats and goodies inside.

i shake my head.

gifts are only given
so they can be used to guilt later;
this is what i have always known.
i have been told no so often;
here i am, standing as a blocker
to my own growth.
for someone to be so sure of my success
makes me doubtful.
i feel the bubbling of anger rise.
i will create justifications for not
reaping the rewards of my hard work.
it hurts to realise
that i was always deserving of good things.
it hurts to know
that my determination is working.
it hurts to know
that there are no fingers to point elsewhere.
i have my hands behind my back
clutched to the doorframe;

i am in my own way;

i am the obstacle i need to overcome.

growing

tell me i am good enough
for the stars and galaxies i dream about.
that there is a ladder waiting
with my name on it.
look into my eyes and see me.
tell me you believe in me.
tell me i am talented enough.
wear the cheerleader costume
i have worn for years.
i know i can start climbing,
but i just need someone to believe in me too,
so i know i am not crazy for thinking
that maybe i could live up there
with the stars
someday.

growing

you can be *anything*,
you can't be <u>everything.</u>

growing

they say to give credit where credit is due, so therefore i want to thank my mother, for always seeing the best in me, even when our viewpoints miss each other. i hope my mother knows how grateful i am for the phone calls, hugs, and guidance and for how safe it feels to be around her even when we sit in silence. i hope my mother knows how much i reminisce about our takeaway nights and dancing in the kitchen, how thankful i am that when i've needed her, she's always been there to listen. i hope she knows how blessed i feel that i can trust her to show up and never have to question how much she cares or her love. i hope my mother knows how much i appreciate her patience when we try to make the pieces fit and how sorry i am for the teenage years full of days where i didn't show it. i hope my mother knows that she's brought calm to storms she doesn't even know about and that she's taught me lessons and effort in ways that i can't live without. i hope she knows i see her progress and that i am proud of her for healing. i hope she knows that i see her sacrifice and that it is because of her that i have a future worth believing in. i hope my mother knows that without her, my dreams would have never stood a chance, and i hope my mother knows that *she is the reason that i have grown to be the person that i am.*

growing

it has taken me twenty-three years to realise
that love does not light your house on fire
and blame you for the flames.
love does not spread hatred
using your name in vain.

love does not lead you into a corner,
placing unwanted hands between your thighs;
love does not use unkind words
until there are tears in your eyes.

love does not seem distant,
saying anything but the truth;
love does not describe these actions;
the label has been misused.

this is not how love is supposed to be;
what you were taught was a lie;
love should be gentle and soft spoken;
love is not hate in disguise.

growing

nobody talks about the grief that comes with meeting the ones who love you properly. the ones who show up over and over and over. the ones who not only notice you, but they see you too. the ones that celebrate your wins and console you during your losses. the ones that unravel the knots and old teachings because not everyone is as big and bad as you thought they were. the ones that help you unlearn and relearn. the ones that make you reflect on all the times when love was unrequited and unreciprocated. the ones that remind you of all the people who made you think their inability to love was somehow intertwined with your worth. the ones that show you how bright the road is ahead, so you stop turning around. the ones that have you grieving who you were, as that version cannot exist through the next chapter. the ones that taught you to work on yourself, not because it's easy, but because you deserve to know how it feels to be cared for. the ones who show you that you were always worth it. the ones that love you so hard that it leads you to grieve all the times you settled for less. the ones who show you what love is, so you will forever know what it isn't.

growing

i still think about that night sometimes.
it was the first time you were so quiet with me.
we didn't talk much,
your tone wasn't the same.
and in that moment,
under my bedroom light at 8:46 p.m,
i realised

that i love you like falling asleep to the sound of rain,
like the smell of cinnamon in autumn,
like listening to the same song on repeat,
like the warmth of a shower in winter.
that i love you so much that i've forgotten what a life without loving you felt like,

and that was *terrifying*.

growing

a chip in my coffee mug,
cracked paint on my dresser,
a rip in my blanket,
a hole in my sweater.
used until they break
pressured until reshaped
to be loved is to be worn.
the marks are evidence that
love remains.

growing

if anyone were to shed a light on my childhood, they would only see you. you helped me become everything i was; you were a stepping stone for everything i am and everything i will be. i know it has been years. we are different people now, and everything has moved on. but i want you to know that despite all of the drifting and deteriorating, *i am so glad that i spent my younger years laughing with you.*

growing

there you were
in the shirt i bought for you,
smiling like you forgot you lost me.
i stood staring,
scared you would turn around and notice me.
i have no idea what i would have said,
knowing you had moved on
while i was trying to forget.
maybe it was right that i ran when i could;
maybe it is stupid
to hope that if i asked you to come back,
you would.
i'll always wonder
if you settled or if you were happy
to be with anyone
or anywhere
that wasn't me.

growing

you don't have to forgive them. you don't have to accept them; you can be angry the rest of your days if you want to, but you deserve to move on from there. you deserve to not repeat the tapes and not live there anymore. you deserve to open your mind to new love, new places, and new perspectives. you do not have to forgive; you can be indifferent. you can learn, grow, heal, and be whoever you like. you don't have to forget or forgive them, but if you can go on in this life as a healthier and happier version of yourself, you are worth a try.

growing

i've been noticed,
seen,
wanted.
maybe this is my chance
things could actually work out for me.

growing

i hope and pray with every bone in my body that our paths cross again, that every star aligns, and that the pieces fall back into place so once again you are by my side. the years pass, and missing you never does. i hope you are living all of the dreams we talked about. i hope your present will become memories we laugh about someday. it is never too late to turn around. i make enough food for two, and my fridge has your favourite juice. i will always save you a seat.

growing

i saw an old man carrying store-bought flowers,
i wondered who they were for.
he made me wonder if love will last until i have
wrinkles, too.

growing

sometimes
i talk to the clouds about you,
wondering if you see me
all the way down here,
asking where all of this
is leading me to.
i would like to think
you are proud of me
for every night i wished on a star
and all the times i worked so hard;
the years do not make it easier.
i miss you;
i wish you were here,

wherever you are.

growing

i have met people who have healed me in
ways they know nothing about.

growing

i collected umbrellas
as it always seemed to rain;
thunderstorms were common
the colours on my clothes would fade.
you walked in
and it has not rained a day since,
i keep the umbrellas just in case,
but i have a feeling
i'm not going to need them again.

growing

you are healing a heart you didn't break. you are soothing wounds that you never made. you have made this mind no longer afraid. you see the beauty in everything i create. i had no idea you were on the way, but my god, you were worth the wait. you are an abundance of sunsets and safety. you have me slowing down my steps instead of panicking, with half a heartbeat racing. i never got the chance to tidy the house and put my best sweater on, but you accepted me regardless of how messy. you helped wash the dishes. you kissed me on the forehead. who knew being whole would start at twenty three. you saw worn and showed how it could fit you perfectly. you are everything i needed and everything i always thought would be a maybe.

growing

if they love you, they will show you. loudly. vibrantly. it will be so obvious to you that there is no shade to hide under. they will not make room for doubt or worries because that space will be used for making plans and remembering how you like your coffee. it will be clear like january skies, and like your morning alarm, you will be reminded about how you make their days a little brighter. if they love you, they will be a safe place from storms, not a constant creator of them. you will not have to be disruptive and explosive to be treated well. if they love you, there will be transparency and vulnerability. if they love you, you will not have to be strategic in how and when you communicate; there will be no obstacle courses or tests for you to earn your basic needs being met. if they love you, excuses will not exist, and promises will be kept. if they love you, support and empathy will not be withheld, and showing up for you will be a given. if they love you, they will accept the person you are and be excited to meet all of the versions of yourself that you'll become. if they love you, they will want you to feel it, and if they love you, you will.

growing

i am rich in many ways—not in the lines of my pockets, in stocks, or in flights booked—but in who and what surrounds me.

i am rich through the people who raised me still being able to breathe; i have a roof over my head and everything i need. i have an abundance of joyful memories and have music at my fingertips that instantly makes me dance and puts my mind at ease. i am rich in how i can reach a better quality of life, and i am rich in the way my fridge is stocked with foods i like. i am rich in my ability to feel and love so deeply and to share that with people who understand me. i am rich in the way i woke up this morning and in the way i get to fall asleep tonight. i am rich in the way that i can look directly at a storm, and without knowing the outcome, i have trust in myself that i'll be alright. i am rich in the way that i get to try new things and to notice how pretty flowers and the sky look in spring. i am rich in the way there is laughter and love in my home. i am rich in the way that i'm so comfortable with myself that i'm not lonely when i'm alone. i am rich in opportunities to have a healthier relationship with myself, and i'm rich in the way that i am blessed to be me, so there's no need to be anybody else. i am rich in the way i have a body that works, and i am rich in the freedom to put myself first. i'm so rich in what matters that materialism isn't even in the picture. i'm rich in the way that i value what i have now, even if one day i'm lucky enough to be richer. i am rich in the simple ways that so many ignore and take for granted. i am rich in my realisation of everything i have been blessed with so that i can water my own grass and appreciate where i've been planted.

growing

no matter how lost
you may feel,
you are always worth
finding again.

growing

the bravest thing i have ever done
was change my mind.

Daffodils

(*new beginnings*)

growing

if there was ever a time when i did not know
what decision to make,
my mother always told me to take three days.
one night, tell yourself that you will do it;
the next night, tell yourself that you will not.
when you wake up on the third day,
you will either feel at peace
or you will feel uneasy.
your body will know what to do,
and when your body tells you what path to take,

start walking.

growing

i knew it was time to go
when the heel of my shoe split.
when i was showing up later,
missing breakfast, and breaking promises.
when my days started with a sigh
and ended with a glass of white wine.
when someone would ask how i was doing,
i would shrug and say, *"it's going okay"*.
i knew it was time to go
when the fuse that used to burn in my chest fizzled
and i could no longer relight my fire.
no matter how many long walks,
podcasts, or recipes i tried.
i knew it was time to go
when my external world was my magnet,
and as long as i stayed standing there,
it would always weigh me down.

growing

start over again
and again, and again.
whenever you need to,
wherever it takes you,
whoever you become
will be worth it.

growing

to be honest,
i have no idea what i want,
but i know what i don't want,
and i think that's a good place to start.

growing

i started watering plants
that have been dying to grow for years;
they have colours
that i have never seen before.
i always thought they were weeds,
a temptation for a life that
would never be mine to reach.
but it turns out
the sun shines brighter now
and the voice gets louder
no matter where i travel to.
maybe it is time
i let myself grow into the person
i have always wanted to be,
let my guard down, and trust that
somewhere there is a puzzle
waiting for a piece
that is shaped
just like *me*.

growing

it is in my healthiest relationships that i have uncovered the most triggers. i have never felt peace like this, but with it has come the exposure of all my suppressed broken pieces. it has presented multiple memories and behaviours to address. it has shed light on the things i have ignored and reopened wounds i didn't think i had to heal from anymore. the awareness of my experiences has knocked me off my feet while keeping me standing still. the gust of wind is not enough to make me fall like it once was. while my healthy relationships remind me, they do not keep me haunted. this time, when i am faced with the weight of my hurt, i am safe. i am supported, and when the rain feels heavy enough to drown all of my hard work out, i have the tools to search for the sun and carve my own silver linings.

growing

i knew as soon as i left
that i wanted to turn around,
but i kept going anyway;
otherwise, i'd be the talk of the town.
initially, it felt right for me,
but quickly came a cold chill.
the sun disappeared for days.
i told myself,
"i may not see it now, but eventually i will".
i was used to noticing every open door
running through each one
out of worry that if i did not catch them,
all my hard work would come undone.
i hid my indecision
so my losses wouldn't create amusement,
but nobody ever learned anything
from a lack of movement.
there is no regret.
i did what i thought was right.
it is better to try and the pieces not fit
than to live the life of someone else
and always wonder
if they might.

growing

i am terrified of being the girl who broke your heart—
the one that couldn't heal enough to be the last.
when i catch myself snapping
or saying something that sounds like them,
i break.
i feel how fragile your heart is;
i see the admiration you have in your eyes
every time i laugh.
i have never been *loved* like this.
i have never been *seen* before.
i worry that this version of me
is not the one who is ready for you.
i realise how much work i have left to do.
i just hope your patience lasts
so i can unlearn and relearn
because i can't be that girl for you.
i can't be the girl who lost you.

growing

soft love has made me sympathetic to the living,
no matter how haunted.

growing

you can leave your keys on the counter,
your shoes by the door,
make yourself comfortable,
you do not need to wear your mask anymore.
there is juice in the fridge,
and a bed for you to lay.
you do not have to have it together,
tomorrow will be a better day.
you have gotten through heavier rain,
this is not the same,
but soon the days will feel lighter
and you will not feel this way.

growing

opening a second bottle of wine
as the christmas tree lights fade.
it has been two and a half years,
and you still look at me the same.
we laugh and dance around the kitchen.
you have given me a life i finally believe in.
"*i love you*," my heart is shouting.
i'll whisper in your ear
that, for the first time in my life,
the only place i am longing to be
is with you
right here.

growing

i notice
the little victories
when i feel myself
on the cliff of a bad habit
and i turn around
to walk in a different direction.
knowing i am strong enough
to undo the knots is something
i am so proud of.

growing

start on a thursday morning
at 9:47am,
begin on a sunday
at 4pm.
learn that changing
does not have a perfect schedule;
let yourself be the person you want to be
without perfecting
when it will be
and when it is your turn.

growing

not all doors need to be walked through.
some serve to let in a breeze;
they show you there's more to the world
than what you can see.
some act as distractions
or temptations of the new.
a chance to know
if your choices align with you.

growing

i always stand back up
that is my superpower.

growing

you'll get over them;
you'll run so far you'll wonder why
it was ever them to begin with.
so much time will pass,
the little reminders won't last.
very soon, they will be a story
you've forgotten you wrote
because you'll realise that these people
might love you more,
but you've got to love yourself the most.

growing

what i'd tell my younger self

i'd tell her it isn't a race, that hers is the only lane, and no matter what direction she goes in, she is always in first place. i'd tell her that she's not running out of time, that life is full of endless combinations, and that she has every day to change her mind. i'd tell her that her feelings are valid and that she has every right to grieve. i'd tell her that she will meet people one day who have the natural reflexes to meet her needs. i'd tell her to slow down when she's weary so she can catch her breath, to make decisions based on what she cares about, and that she will find healthy ways to handle the rest. i'd tell her that the heaviness gets lighter and that there are still so many colours to see. i'd tell her that this world is vast enough to embrace *anything* and *everything* she wants to be.

growing

you are going to miss this.

the freedom in your indecision, the last-minute adventures, the childlike laughter, your first apartment's kitchen. the proximity of your friends. the summer days that don't end. quality time with your parents. scribbling on maps, circling the places you have been. the concerts, the dancing, the dreaming, and the late talking. the way you don't have to run because you have plenty of time for walking. having a multitude of options and deciding on some. the spontaneity of your choices when your life feels like it's coming undone.

the memories you're making outweighing the money you spent. do not miss what is abundantly in front of you by fixating on what is ahead,

because eventually, time takes hold and what once was tomorrow becomes 40 years ago.

you are going to miss this: the ability to devote yourself to whatever you put your mind to,

so do not let your wishes for possible difference

steal away your chance to experience your present view.

growing

you are worthy of love now. your heart does not need to be fully intact to warrant someone giving you that. you do not need to be fully healed to be treated better. you do not need to have it all figured out and have everything together. you can do the work; you can soothe the scars, but since day one, you have always been worth loving for exactly who you are. there are no past versions of yourself needing to compete; you don't need to wait until you're complete. there is no checklist you have to work through before you have earned all of the love you have always deserved. you deserved it a year ago, yesterday, and now, and if you ever feel too lost for love, i promise you, you have always deserved to be found.

growing

the older i get, the more i am reminded that home is no longer yellow kitchen walls and a designated street sign. i thought it would fade with the sale of my childhood house or when i packed my last box for university. i thought it was lost when my mother moved again and my new bedroom didn't feel as warm as the last. i thought home was buried in the walls of my teenage wardrobe and drilled into the floorboards of my last apartment. home was materialistic; it was the physical attributes of a particular walking route, a coffee shop, and a weekend ritual takeaway that i associated with being at home. as i have grown up, my sense of home has shifted and split between places. home became more than glimpses of nostalgia for a place i have outgrown; it's in hearts that beat within it. it remains in every catch-up phone call and playing old country songs. home is the feeling of security and peace that i feel around those i love. it's in the familiarity of cooking childhood recipes and making my friends laugh. home is the invisible string between trust and the innocence of my childhood. now that i am older, home is a lighthouse. when i rock the boat, the people i love shine their light to remind me that no matter how far i have gone, there is somewhere fixed to provide warmth and understanding, and that no matter the fog, there is always somewhere to swim back to. when i am homesick, it is never for cobbled streets and creaking stairs anymore; i am homesick for the presence of people who have made growing up something to be nurtured and treated fruitfully. *i now know that even through loss and change, home is never really gone; it remains in the hearts of those i love.*

growing

do i know what i want to do with my life?

absolutely not.

life is long. life is short. life is tiring. life is unpredictable and constantly changing. i am not who i was a year ago, and a year from now, i will say the same thing. i have changed my mind more times than i can count, and with each, i have learned more about myself. it is not about knowing; it is about trying things. failing over and over. falling down five times and getting back up a sixth time. it is about walking in one direction and, when the tide changes, listening to it and turning around. i have overcome and undone so much healing in this year alone, and i will start and stop all over again in the next. all i am saying is that i give myself permission to make choices that align with the kind of person i want to be. i give myself permission to be alive and present, even when the definition of that is constantly being rewritten.

so, do i know what i want to do with my life?

absolutely not.

growing

sunflowers on the windowsill,
toast with strawberry jam—
in this moment,
i am okay with not knowing what is next
or the time taken to learn who i am.
right now,
it is just me
and the summer heat.
these days are slow,
but will carry my body
wherever and whenever
it needs to be.

thank you note ♡

this book would not exist without these wonderful people:

my book cover artist, Kate Hall Design (@kate_hall_design) : thank you for helping me bring my book to life with your art. you are incredibly talented and were a joy to work with.

my editor, Emily Price Soli: thank you for your kindness and dedication when handling my work. you helped me shape how i wanted to tell my story in such a considerate and mindful way. thank you for being so caring when guiding the narrative of this book.

my friends: thank you for being so supportive and excited for me. your words of encouragement and reassurance aided the creation of this book more than you know.

my partner: thank you for being such a rock through the creative process. you were a listening ear and embodied every way to be supportive through every moment of creating this book. you are one of the reasons that this book has become what it is today. thank you for being <u>you.</u>

my mother: my cheerleader from the very beginning. thank you for supporting me from writing this book to everything you did before that led me here. you have championed me through every aspect of my life. thank you for *everything.*

    & thank *you* for reading my work. your support means everything to me.

    thank you for being here.

you can find more of my work at
@katiececiliapoetry on tiktok and instagram.

www.katiececiliapoetry.com

Printed in Dunstable, United Kingdom